T0086588

DVD Classical Guitar

Written by Chad Johnson and Doug Boduch

Video Performer: Doug Boduch

ISBN: 978-1-4234-9490-4

HAL•LEONARD®
CORPORATION
7777 W. BLUEMOUND RD. P.O. BOX 13819 MILWAUKEE, WI 53213

Visit Hal Leonard Online at
www.halleonard.com

Table of Contents

Introduction **3**

LESSON 1 . . . . **4**

Playing Position

Rest Stroke and Free Stroke
"ODE TO JOY" – Ludwig Van Beethoven
"BRIDAL CHORUS" – Richard Wagner

Combining the Thumb and Fingers
"ODE TO JOY" – Ludwig Van Beethoven
"SARABANDE" – Arcangelo Corelli
"ANDANTINO IN C" – Mateo Carcassi
"WALTZ IN D" – Ferdinando Carulli
"WALTZ (OP. 39, NO. 15)" – Johannes Brahms
"RONDO IN C (OP. 241, NO. 25)" – Ferdinando Carulli

LESSON 2 . . . .**12**

Chord Technique
"ODE TO JOY" – Ludwig Van Beethoven

Adding the Thumb
"MINUET IN C" – Mateo Carcassi
"STUDY #1 IN C (OP. 6, NO. 8)" – Fernando Sor
"STUDY #3 (OP. 35)" – Fernando Sor
"BARCAROLLE" – Napoléon Coste

Left Hand Slur Technique
"SLUR STUDY IN C" – Ferdinando Carulli
"ALLEGRO SPIRITOSO (OP. 10, NO. 10)" – Mauro Giuliani
"ODE TO JOY" – Ludwig Van Beethoven
"WALTZ OF THE ROBINS (OP. 44, NO. 3)" – Fernando Sor
"STUDY IN E (OP. 6, NO. 3)" – Fernando Sor

LESSON 3 . . . .**22**

Sustaining Bass Notes
"MINUET IN G" – Johann Sebastian Bach
"BOUREE IN E MINOR" – Johann Sebastian Bach
"STUDY #6 (OP. 60)" – Mateo Carcassi
"RONDO ALLEGRETTO" – Mateo Carcassi

Barre Technique

Arpeggios
"CAPRICCIO IN C MAJOR (OP. 26, NO. 1)" – Mateo Carcassi
"STUDY IN B MINOR (OP. 35, NO. 22)" – Fernando Sor
"PRELUDE IN D MINOR" – Ferdinando Carulli
"MODERATO IN E MINOR" – Mauro Giuliani
"STUDY IN E MINOR (OP. 6, NO. 11)" – Fernando Sor

Vibrato
"ROMANCE IN E MINOR" – Anonymous

INTRODUCTION

Welcome to *DVD Classical Guitar*, from Hal Leonard's exciting At a Glance series. Not as in-depth and slow-paced as traditional method books, the material in *DVD Classical Guitar* is presented in a snappy and fun manner intended to have you playing in the classical style in virtually no time at all. Plus, the At a Glance series uses real songs by real composers to illustrate how the concepts you're learning are applied. For example, in *DVD Classical Guitar*, you'll learn J.S. Bach's "Minuet in G" and Beethoven's "Ode to Joy," among many others.

Additionally, each book in the At a Glance series comes with a DVD containing video lessons that correspond to the printed material. The DVD that accompanies this book contains three video lessons, each approximately 8 to 10 minutes in length, which correspond to each chapter. In these videos, ace instructor Doug Boduch will show you in great detail everything from right-hand technique to dressing up your melodies with vibrato. As you work through this book, try to play the examples first on your own; then check out the DVD for additional help or to see if you played it correctly. As the saying goes, "A picture is worth a thousand words." So be sure to use this invaluable tool on your quest to mastering classical guitar.

LESSON 1

Classical guitar is played on a nylon-string acoustic and involves plucking the strings with the right-hand fingers, as opposed to playing with a pick. This technique allows you to play both a melody and an accompaniment at the same time. There are a few formalities that differ from playing a standard guitar, so let's discuss those first.

Playing Position

The first thing to take note of is how to sit and hold the classical guitar. Watch the DVD to see this. You'll want to sit up straight on the edge of your chair and either use a footstool or a guitar support, resting the instrument on the left leg. This puts the guitar in the optimum playing position. If you're used to playing with the guitar resting on your right leg, this new position will take some getting used to.

Left-Hand Position

As far as left-hand position goes, there really is no difference between standard guitar and classical guitar, except for maybe an emphasis to really play with the left hand fingertips, since we'll need to sustain notes while having other strings ring clearly. You'll want to avoid keeping the thumb on top of the neck, as you might do on the electric guitar.

Right-Hand Position

The right hand is where we notice a big difference. But before we take a look at right-hand position, let's discuss how we label the right hand fingers. Since we use numbers for the left hand, we opt to use letters on the right so the two hand fingerings don't get mixed up.

P I M A

The letters we use for the right hand are *p, i, m,* and *a* for the thumb, index, middle, and ring fingers, respectively. These come from the Spanish names for the fingers: *pulgar* for thumb, *indicio* for index, *medio* for middle, and *anular* for ring.

Watch the DVD for proper positioning of the right hand—arched wrist with curved fingertips. Your wrist should be elevated a few inches from the guitar's top.

If you choose to play with the fingernails, which is the accepted way to play classical guitar, your nails should be just a bit longer than your fingertips.

Take some time to file your nails and make sure they're smooth. It's still possible to play without using the fingernails, but your tone will suffer.

Rest Stroke and Free Stroke

So now let's talk about how we pluck the strings. There are two types of right hand strokes in classical guitar: *rest stroke* and *free stroke*. A rest stroke is simply where, after plucking the string with a somewhat downward motion into the guitar, our finger comes to rest on the next string.

To achieve the best tone, you'll want to pluck slightly across the string. Experiment with alternating the fingers. Try i-m, m-a, and i-a.

Here's a popular melody played with all rest strokes: Beethoven's "Ode to Joy."

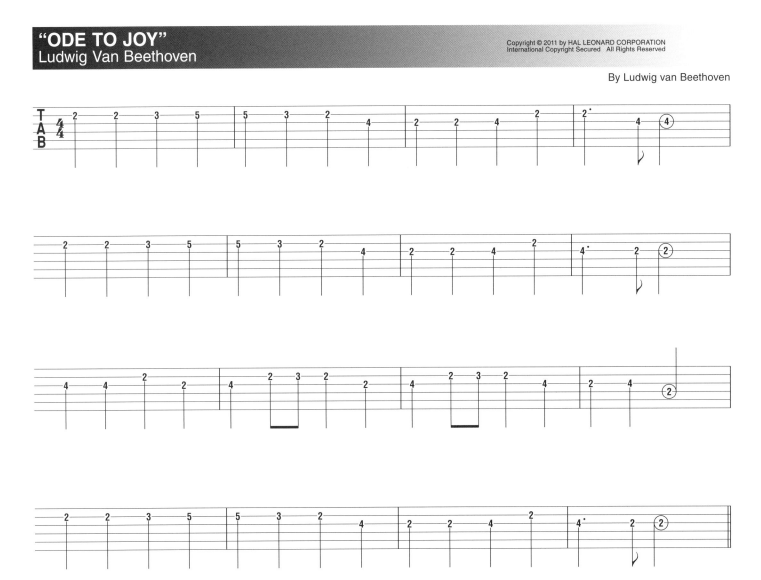

"ODE TO JOY"
Ludwig Van Beethoven

By Ludwig van Beethoven

The basic movements of the free stroke are similar to the rest stroke except in the final phase. Instead of coming to rest, the finger just clears the adjacent string and stops in the air above it.

Try the same Beethoven melody above, only this time using all free strokes.

Let's try another melody now—Wagner's "Bridal Chorus." Try this one with both rest and free strokes.

"BRIDAL CHORUS" from LOHENGRIN
Richard Wagner

By Richard Wagner

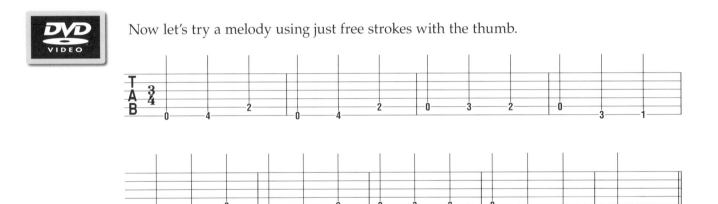

We can also use both free strokes and rest strokes with the thumb. You may be asking yourself why we need these two different strokes. Check out the example on the DVD, and you'll instantly be able to tell. Each stroke produces a different tone. The rest stroke is more full bodied and would be used whenever a melody stands alone, giving it a richer tone. The free stroke will generally be used when combining melody and bass notes, since we wouldn't want to dampen any ringing strings by using a rest stroke.

Now let's try a melody using just free strokes with the thumb.

Here's another bass melody to practice with the thumb. When you play this one with rest strokes, you'll notice another benefit. In measure 3, we play the open A string. This occurs immediately after playing the open D string at the end of measure 2. When you use rest strokes for instances such as this, your thumb will come to rest on the D string, thereby muting it just as the open A string is plucked. This helps keep the bass line sounding crisp and clear. Try the same phrase with free strokes, and you'll hear the difference.

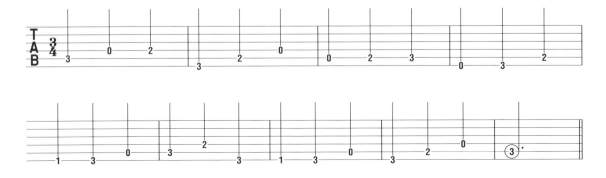

Combining the Thumb and Fingers

The real magic of the classical guitar happens when we play a bass line along with a melody, giving the illusion of two guitars playing at once. You'll want to make sure that the thumb and fingers play the notes at the same time. Here's a quick exercise.

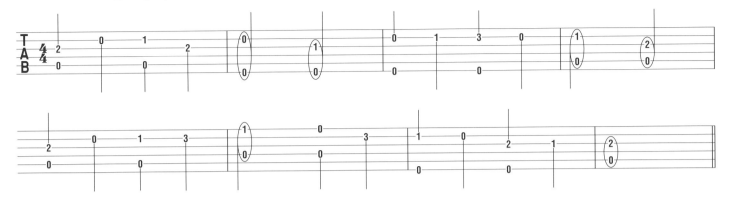

And here's an example in 3/4 where we're playing simultaneous bass and melody notes throughout. Even though the bass is moving quite a bit here, the coordination is pretty simple because you're playing in a 1:1 relationship—one bass note for each melody note.

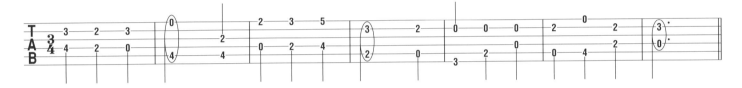

Now let's add some bass notes to our Beethoven melody.

"ODE TO JOY"
Ludwig Van Beethoven

By Ludwig van Beethoven

Let's play a few more pieces to get used to combining bass and treble parts. Though "Sarabande," by Arcangelo Corelli, requires a few position shifts, with a little experimentation regarding the fret-hand fingering, the piece is actually not too difficult.

"SARABANDE"
Arcangelo Corelli

By Arcangelo Corelli

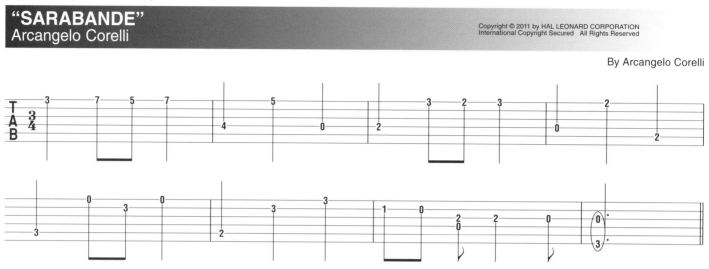

In this excerpt from "Andantino in C," by Mateo Carcassi, we're interjecting the open G string in between treble and bass notes played together. Strive for a smooth, connected sound here, with all the notes speaking equally well.

"ANDANTINO IN C"
Mateo Carcassi

By Mateo Carcassi

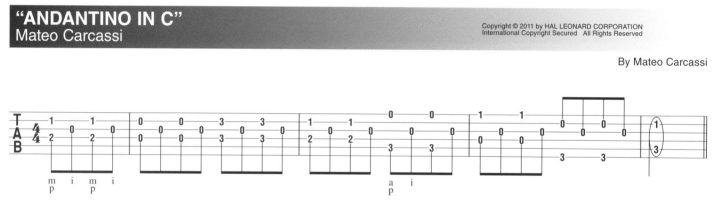

In this next excerpt, from Ferdinando Carulli's "Waltz in D," you'll get plenty of practice with *i*, *m*, and *a*, as the melody moves all around strings 1–3.

"WALTZ IN D"
Ferdinando Carulli

By Ferdinando Carulli

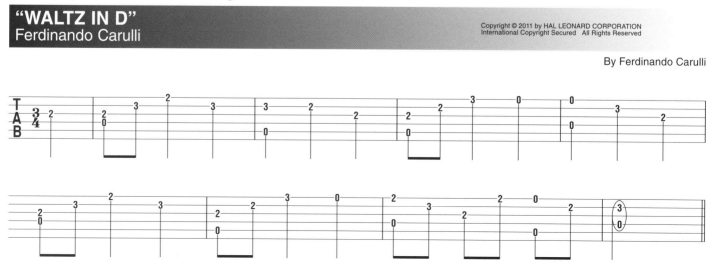

And here's a waltz by Johannes Brahms that's great practice for independence in your right hand. Pay attention to the right-hand fingerings indicated in the music.

"WALTZ, OP. 39"
Johannes Brahms

By Johannes Brahms

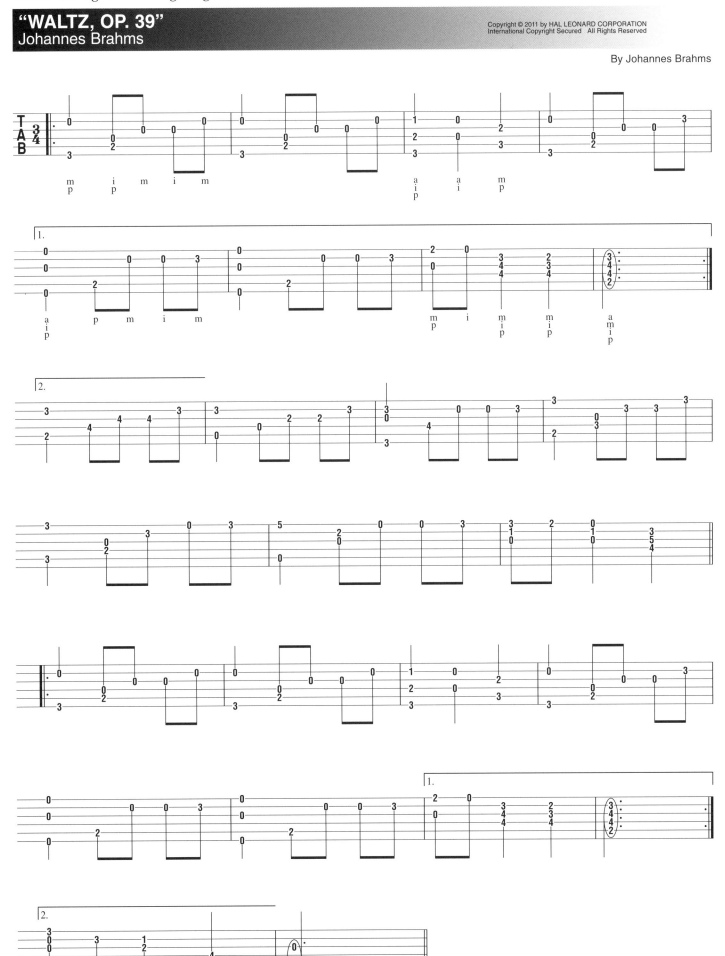

This rondo by Ferdinando Carulli will work every aspect of your technique thus far. Use rest strokes for the chromatic pick-up phrases.

"RONDO IN C, OP. 241, NO. 25"
Ferdinando Carulli

By Ferdinando Carulli

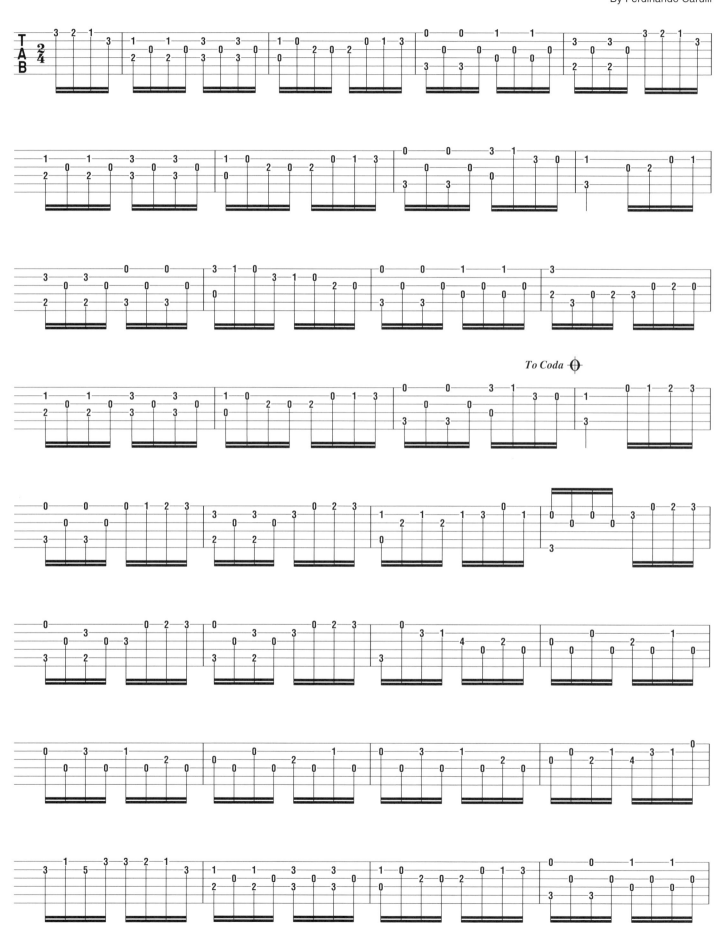

To Coda ⊕

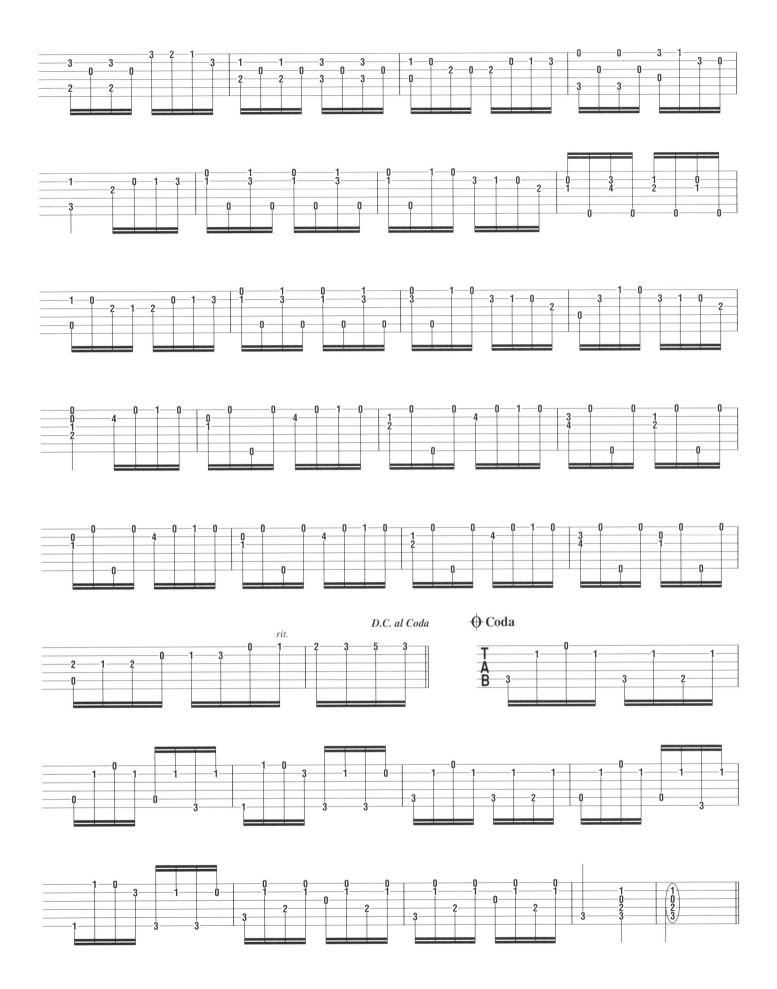

Well, that's it for the lesson. With this introduction to classical guitar, you're on your way to discovering the many joys and challenges that lay ahead.

LESSON 2

In this lesson, we'll continue to explore the classical style with more techniques to broaden your repertoire and expand your tonal palette.

Chord Technique

 When two or more notes are played simultaneously, we refer to it as a *chord*. The technique used for chords will be free strokes with both fingers and thumb. In this next example, we'll use the *i* and *m* fingers to play the notes together. Make sure both notes are sounding at the same time.

Here's another example using just two-note chords, or *dyads*. In this one, try using the *m* and *a* fingers when moving to the 1-2 string group. Otherwise, you can get by with all *i* and *m*.

 When you play these chords, your hand should not move up and down as you pluck the notes. The wrist remains stable, and the movement should come from the finger joints. Now let's take our popular Beethoven melody from the first lesson and play it in chord form. You should also try playing these chords with the *m* and *a* fingers.

"ODE TO JOY"
Ludwig Van Beethoven

By Ludwig van Beethoven

Adding the Thumb

In addition to playing chords with our fingers, we can also add the thumb and incorporate a bass note. This will give the chord a fuller and more complete sound. When adding the thumb, it becomes more difficult to get the notes to speak at the same time, so pay close attention to make sure all notes sound simultaneously.

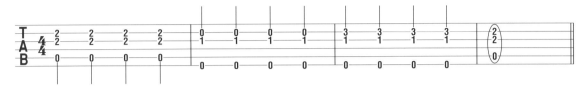

Be sure that all the notes are sounding clearly and at the same volume. It's common for the thumb or the fingers to overpower the other in the beginning. Concentrate on getting all the fingers to transfer equal energy to the strings at the same time.

Here's an excerpt from "Minuet in C" by Carcassi that puts a lot of this together with melody and chords.

"MINUET IN C"
Mateo Carcassi

By Mateo Carcassi

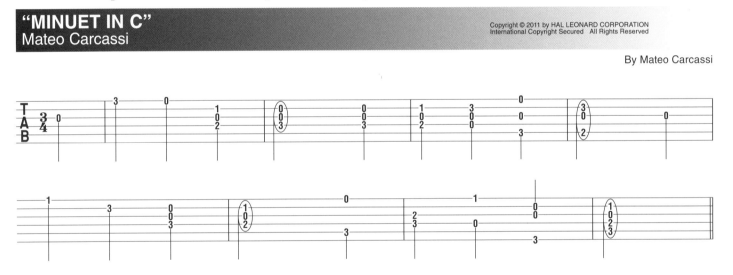

Now let's try out some chords with a more mobile bass line in a short excerpt from "Fernando Sor's Study #1 (Op. 6, No. 8)" in C major. You'll need to shift up to third position in measure 2.

"STUDY #1 IN C, OP. 6, NO. 8"
Fernando Sor

By Fernando Sor

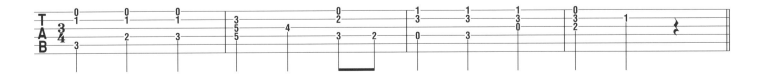

In Sor's "Study #3 (Op. 35)," we'll be mixing in the occasional single note among the dyads on top and using mostly open-string bass notes.

"STUDY #3, OP. 35"
Fernando Sor

By Fernando Sor

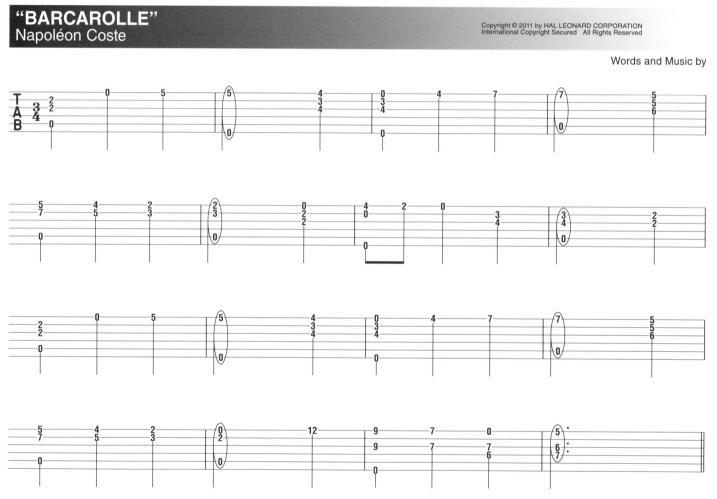

And here's a nice piece by Napoléon Coste that features some lateral movement up the fretboard. Take your time with the shifts to make them nice and smooth.

"BARCAROLLE"
Napoléon Coste

Words and Music by

Left Hand Slur Technique

Sometimes it's desirable to link two notes together in a way that is smoother than simply plucking both of them. When linked this way, the notes are said to be *slurred*. In the music notation, they're connected with a curved line. We'll look at two types of slurs—the upward slur and the downward slur. If you're familiar with other guitar techniques, this is essentially a hammer-on or a pull-off.

In the case of an upward slur, or *hammer-on*, we pluck the first note and hammer down with our next finger to sound the second note.

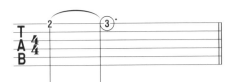

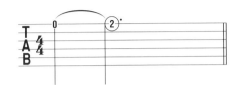
We can do this from an open note as well.

In the case of a downward slur, or *pull-off*, we strike the first note and then pull our finger off the string in a downward motion to sound the second note.

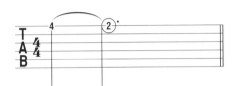

Notice that, with a pull-off, both fingers need to be on the string before plucking.

We can also do a downward slur to an open note.

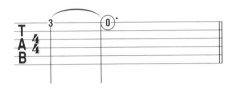

Now let's try some slurs in a short piece.

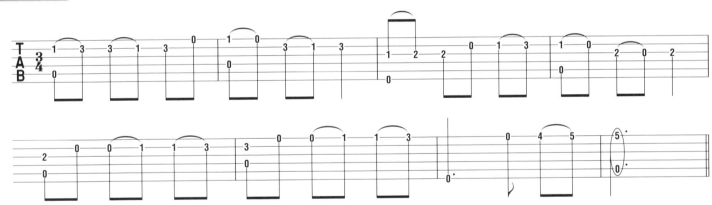

Here's another piece that works on slurring different strings. Make sure you're not rushing or dragging through the slurs. The tempo should stay even throughout.

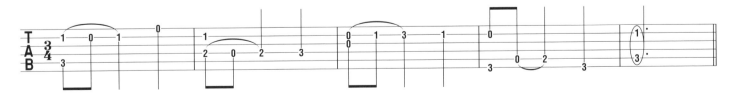

Slur technique takes some time to develop, so here's a great exercise to get you in shape. It works all the different fingers in both upward and downward slurs. The DVD features a demonstration on just one string, but you should work through the pattern on all the strings.

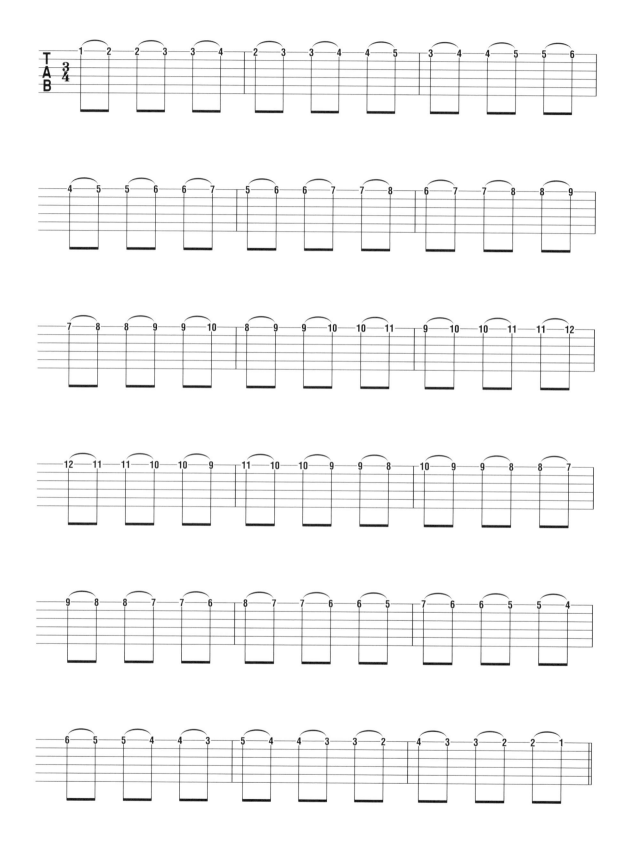

And here's another exercise that works the non-adjacent fingers: 1 and 4, 1 and 3, and 2 and 4. Be sure to stay in one position throughout the exercise so you're working each finger. When performed in first position, as shown here, the tab numbers will also represent which fret-hand finger you should be using as well. After you get through the exercise in first position, shift up to second position and so on, continuing on until you reach eighth or ninth position.

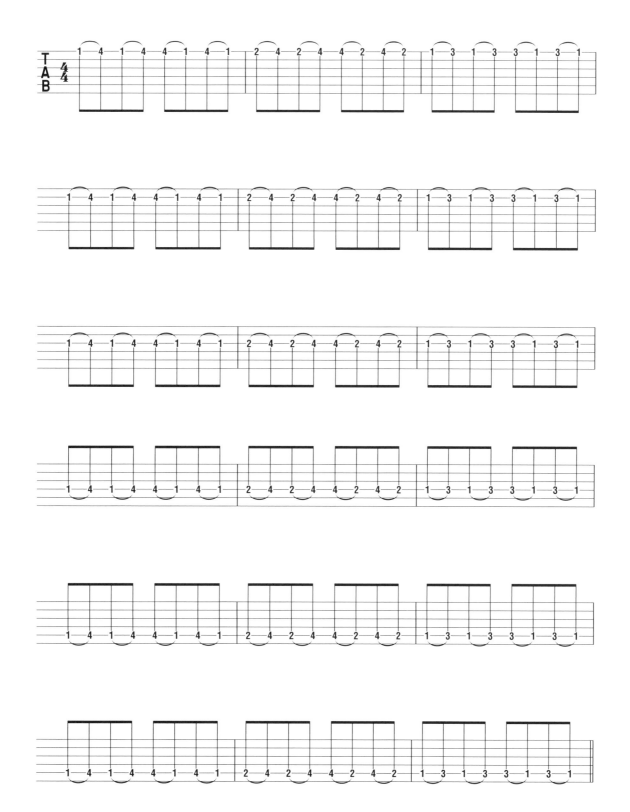

Here's a piece by Ferdinando Carulli that'll really give you a slur workout.

"SLUR STUDY IN C"
Ferdinando Carulli

By Ferdinando Carulli

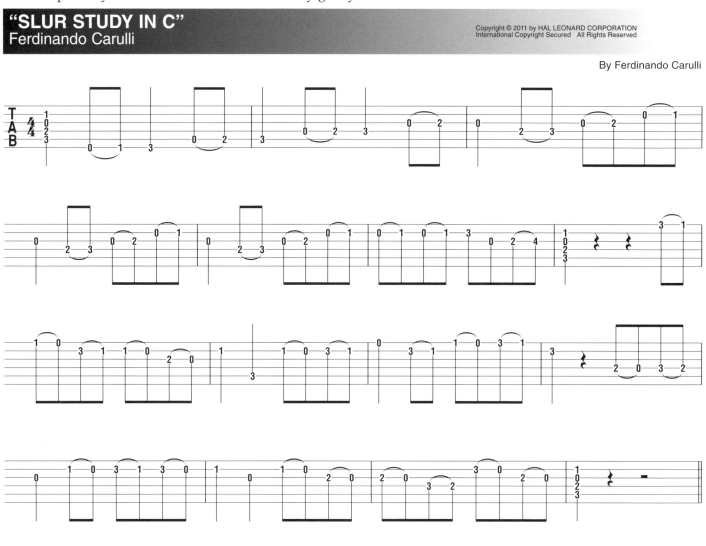

And here's one by Mauro Giuliani, "Allegro Spiritoso (Op. 10, No. 10)," that works out several different finger combinations with a nice melody.

"ALLEGRO SPIRITOSO"
Mauro Giuliani

By Mauro Giuliani

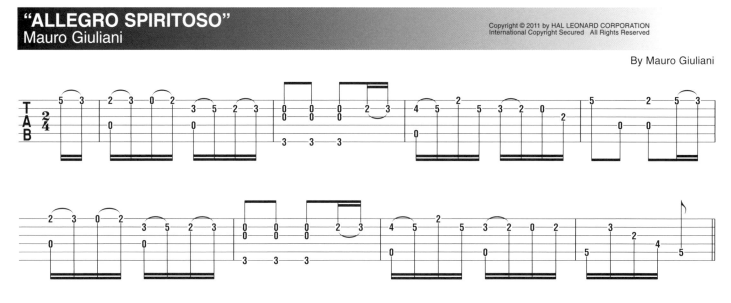

Now we'll take our famous Beethoven melody and play it with our new techniques—chords with bass notes and slurs.

"ODE TO JOY"
Ludwig Van Beethoven

By Ludwig van Beethoven

Fernando Sor's "Waltz of the Robins" is a graceful piece in C to practice your slurs on. It's not very difficult and still sounds nice.

"WALTZ OF THE ROBINS, OP. 44, NO. 3"
Fernando Sor

By Fernando Sor

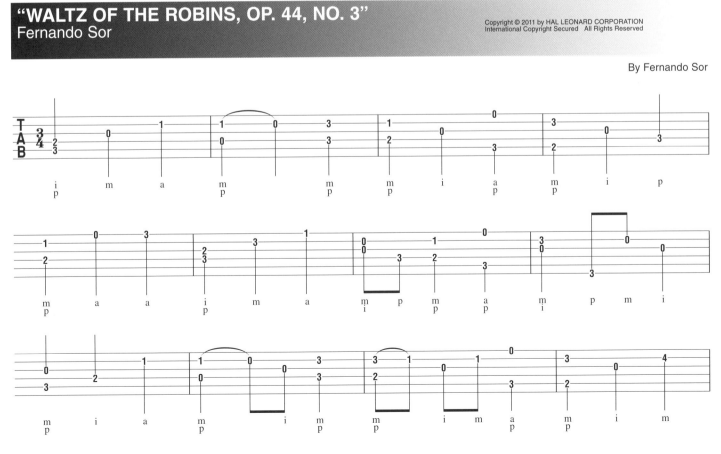

In Sor's "Study in E (Op. 6, No. 3)," you'll practice consecutive downward slurs (or pull-offs) only, coupled with some brisk position shifts.

"STUDY IN E, OP. 6, NO. 3"
Fernando Sor

By Fernando Sor

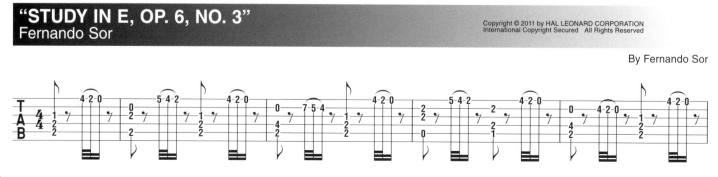

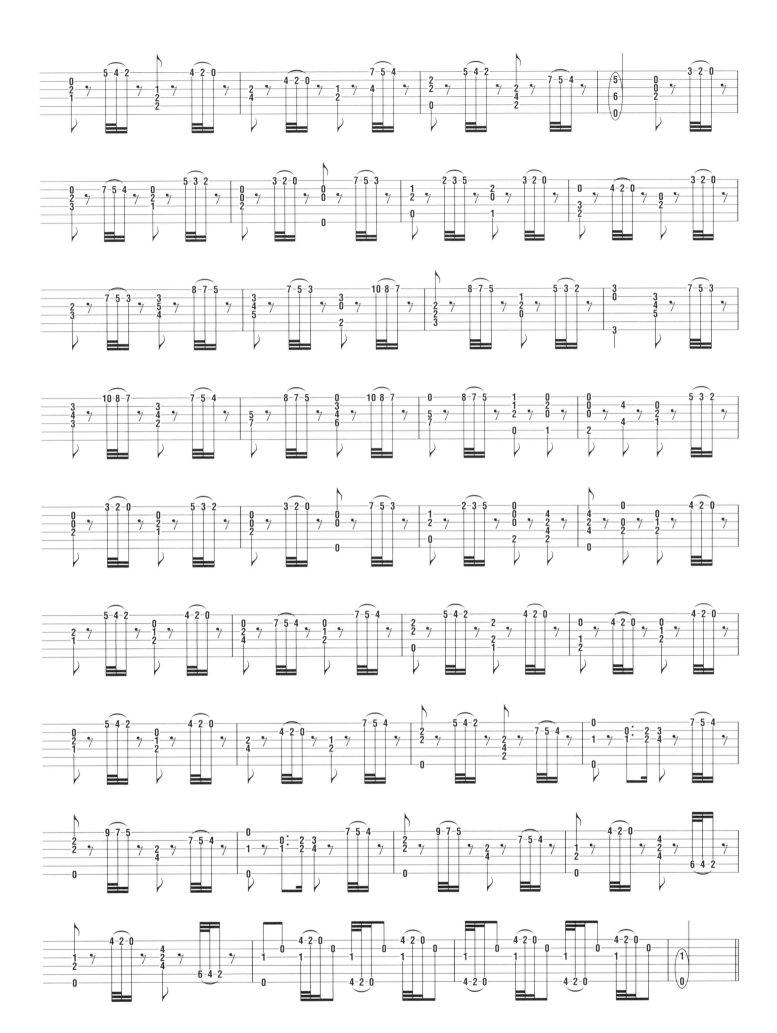

That brings us to the end of this lesson. Be sure to work on these specific techniques in isolation if necessary until you're comfortable with them. Relaxation is key in maintaining a good tone and steady tempo. And that relaxation comes with practice!

LESSON 3

In this lesson, we'll explore some of the finer elements of classical guitar along with learning some great pieces.

Sustaining Bass Notes

If you worked through the first two classical guitar lessons, you saw how we introduced bass notes that would sustain over a melody. Many of these bass notes were open notes. In this lesson, we'll concentrate more on fretted bass notes. These will be more difficult, as we'll need to keep our finger down in order to allow the bass note to sustain. Try it here in a short exercise.

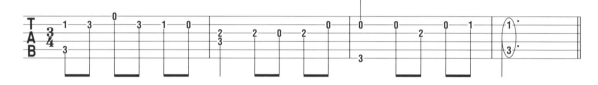

Make sure you keep the bass notes ringing as long as you can over the melody notes. Here's another example where the bass notes change a bit more quickly.

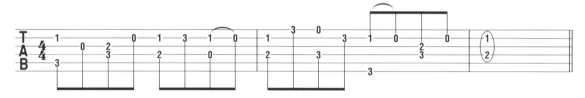

Bach's "Minuet in G" makes great use of sustained bass notes.

"MINUET IN G MAJOR"
Johann Sebastian Bach

By Johann Sebastian Bach

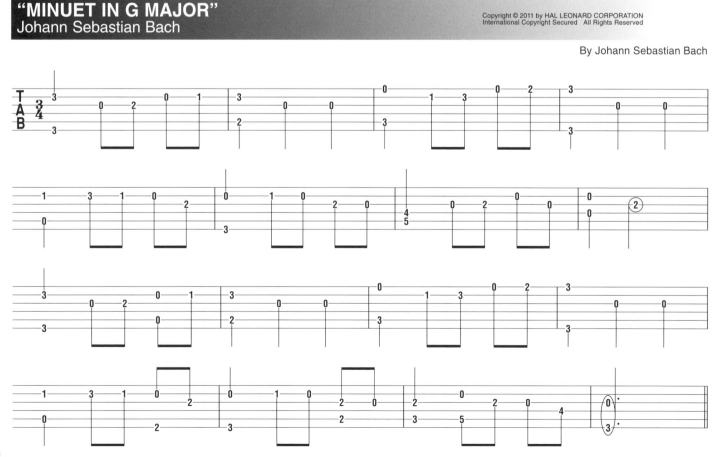

And here's another great Bach piece to practice combining bass and melody notes. You'll get practice with playing bass and melody notes together as well as sustaining bass notes underneath a melody here. Take this one slowly at first, as there are several twists and turns.

"BOURRÈE IN E MINOR" from LUTE SUITE IN E MINOR
Johann Sebastian Bach

By Johann Sebastian Bach

In Carcassi's Study #6 (Op. 60), we're turning the tables a bit with an active bass melody and sparse treble notes.

"STUDY NO. 6, OP. 60"
Mateo Carcassi

By Matteo Carcassi

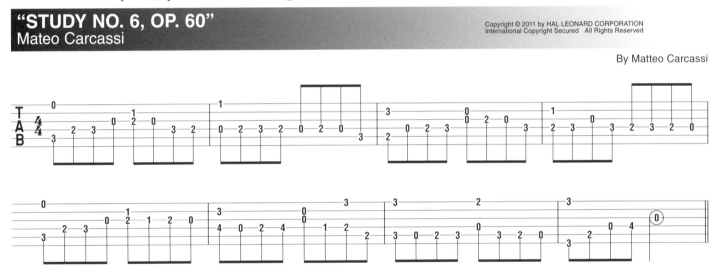

Here's another Carcassi piece that's a lot of fun. Though the bass notes start out as open strings, some fretted ones crop up toward the end, so be ready.

"RONDO ALLEGRETTO"
Mateo Carcassi

By Mateo Carcassi

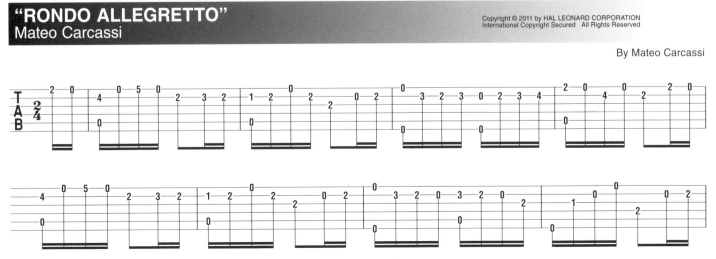

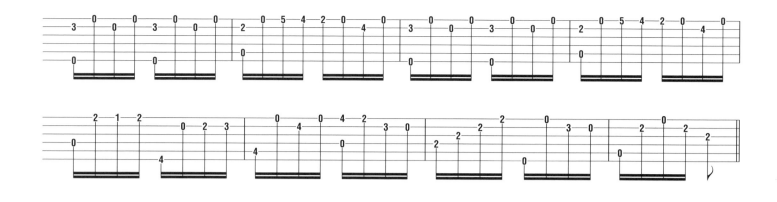

Barre Technique

Sometimes you will encounter a piece that requires you to fret more than one string with one finger. This is referred to as a *barre* and requires that you lay your finger down flat on the fretboard to cover the appropriate number of strings. A barre can be anywhere from just two strings to all six. Try it here on the 5th fret with just two strings.

The important things to remember for achieving a good barre are to keep your finger straight and to use the weight of your left arm for pressure. It helps to roll the finger a bit to the thumb side, as the finger has less of a tendency to bend there. You don't need to have a death grip between the thumb and fingers. Think of pulling the guitar in to you using your shoulder and the weight of your arm.

In the music, a barre will be indicated with a symbol (₵II) where the Roman numeral indicates the fret at which we barre. Now let's try a piece using our barre technique.

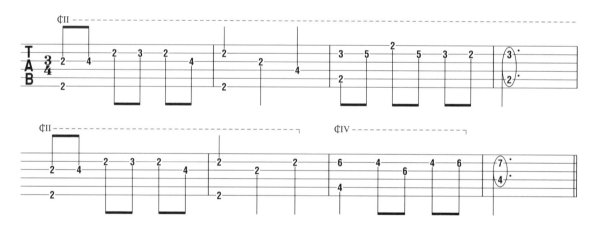

Here's another piece that uses a *partial barre*. We're only barring from string 4 up to string 1 here.

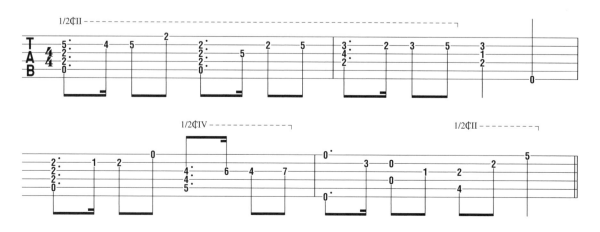

Arpeggios

Arpeggios are simply the notes of a chord played separately. In classical guitar, it becomes a challenge for the right hand, as we'll need to use different fingers for each string. Pay close attention to the right hand fingering in this next example.

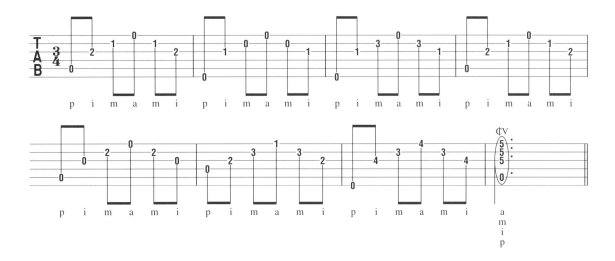

Notice how the left-hand fingers are kept down so all the notes could ring together. There are a ton of great right hand arpeggio studies for the classical guitar. You should seek them out, as this will pay great dividends with your right hand development.

Carcassi's "Capriccio in C Major (Op. 26, No. 1)" is a nice, gentle piece that'll give you lots of practice with ascending arpeggios. There are a few barres in this excerpt as well, so be prepared for them.

"CAPRICCIO IN C MAJOR, OP. 26, NO. 1"
Mateo Carcassi

By Mateo Carcassi

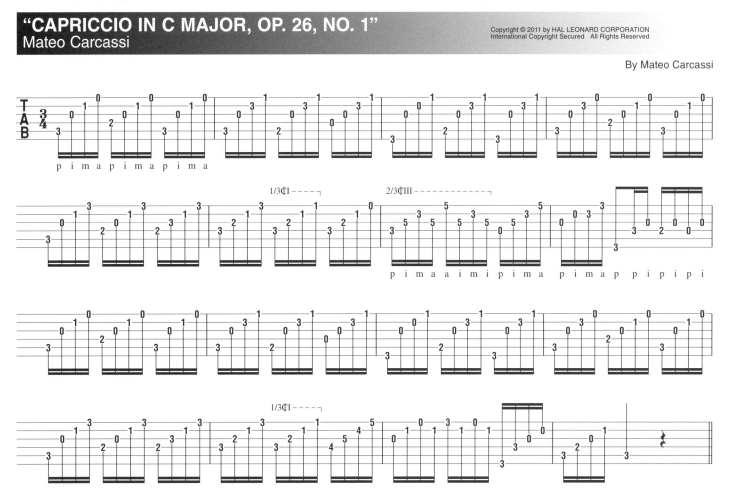

Fernando Sor's "Study in B Minor (Op. 35, No. 22)" is a beautiful arpeggio piece that makes use of several different barres, both full and partial. Pay close attention to the barre markings, as they're integral to achieving a smooth, flowing sound.

"STUDY IN B MINOR"
Fernando Sor

By Fernando Sor

Carulli's "Prelude in D Minor" is a triplet-based arpeggio piece. Make sure the notes are evenly spaced throughout this excerpt.

"PRELUDE IN D MINOR"
Ferdinando Carulli

By Ferdinando Carulli

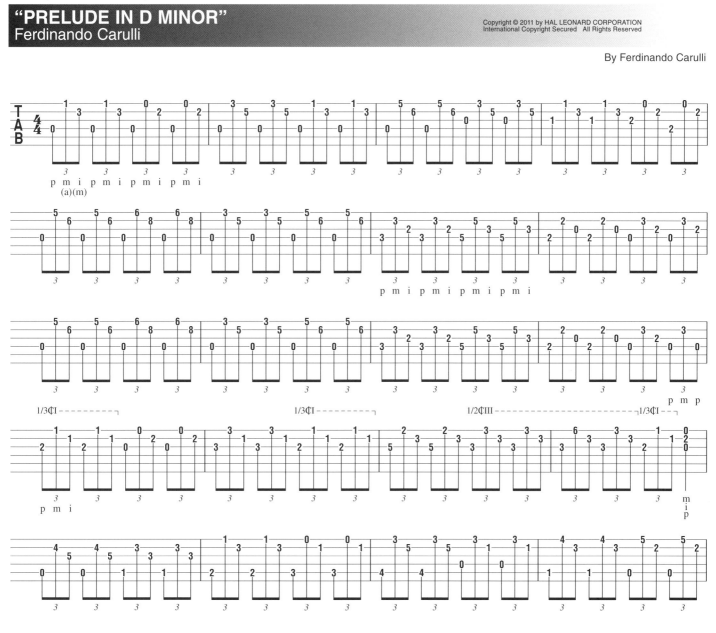

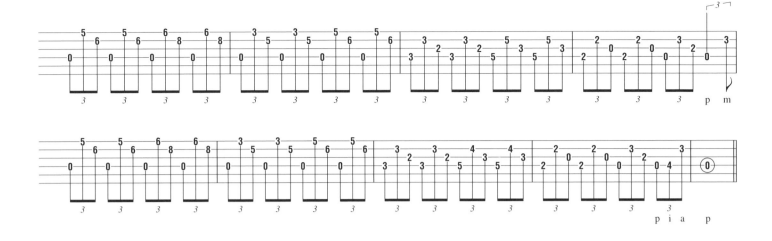

In this etude, "Moderato in E Minor," by Mauro Giuliani, we see a different arpeggio pattern in triplets. The entire piece is presented here, so be sure to dissect it into smaller phrases when learning it.

"MODERATO IN E MINOR"
Mauro Giuliani

By Mauro Giuliani

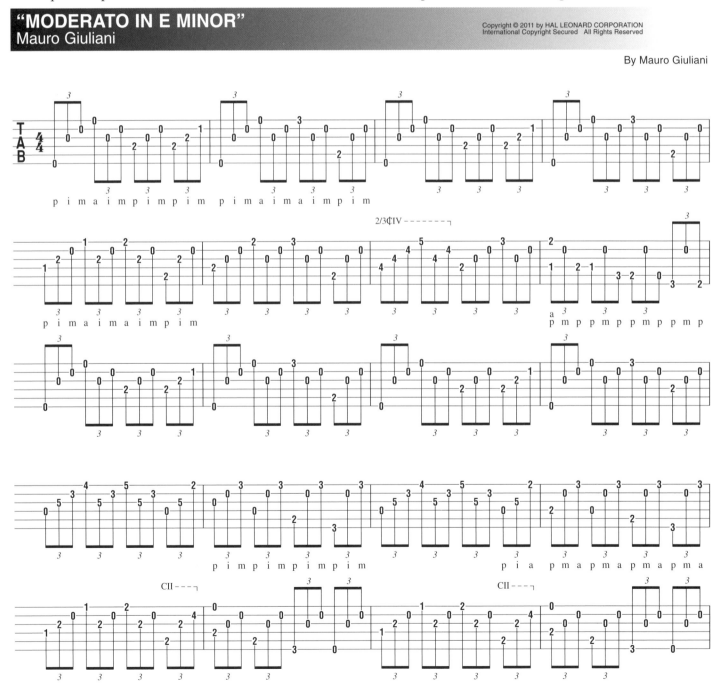

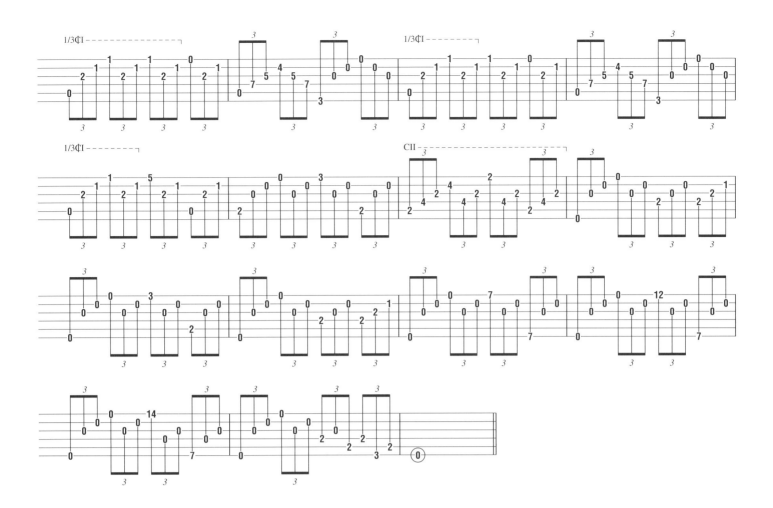

This Sor study presents an extensive arpeggio workout. It's long and contains some tricky chord shaps, so take it slowly and work through it in pieces.

"STUDY IN E MINOR, OP. 6, NO. 11"
Fernando Sor

By Fernando Sor

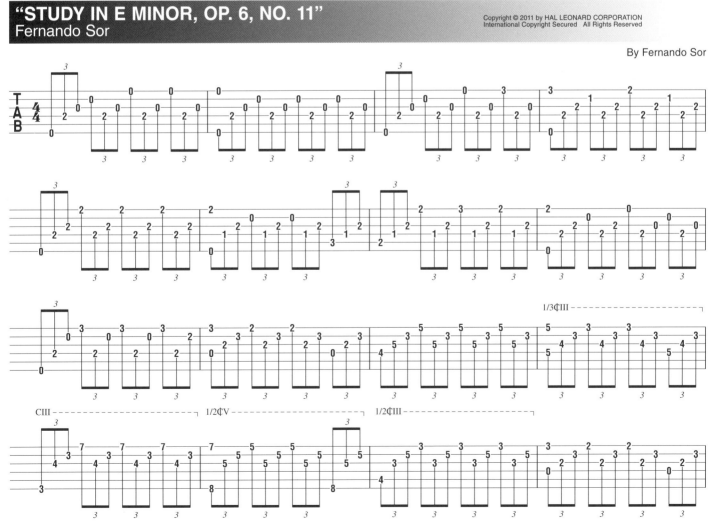

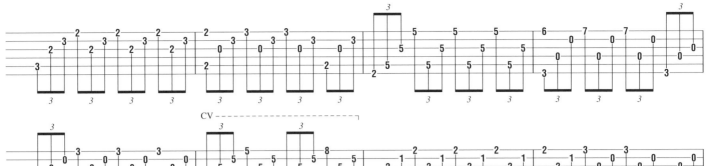

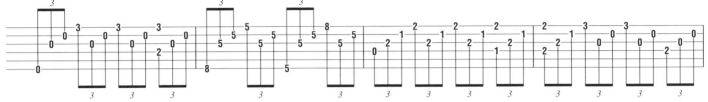

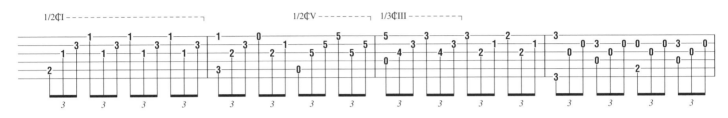

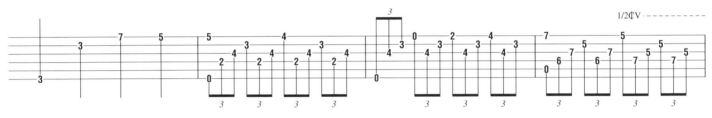

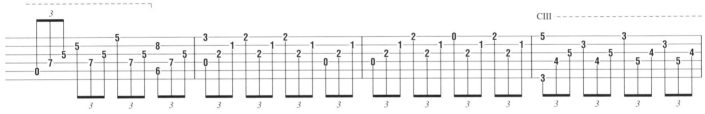

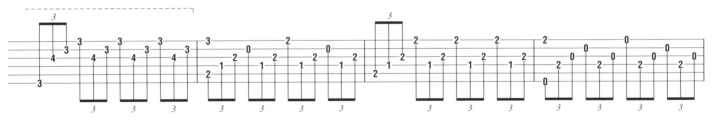

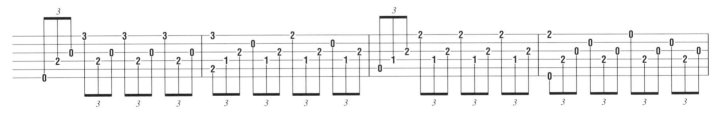

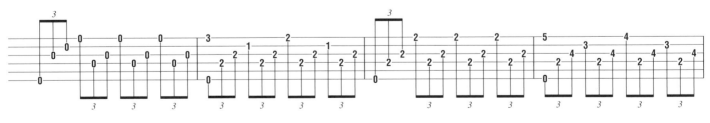

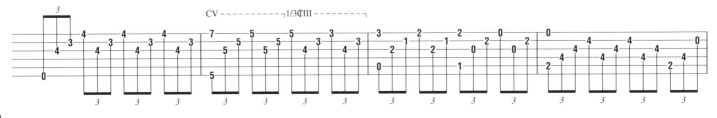

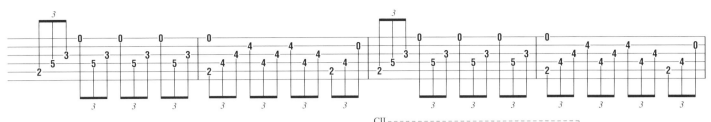

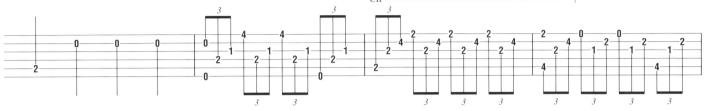

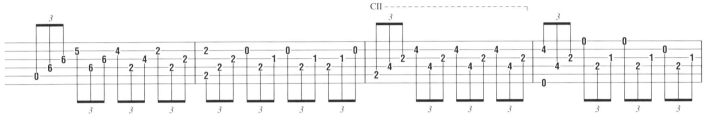

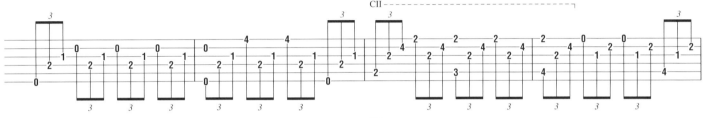

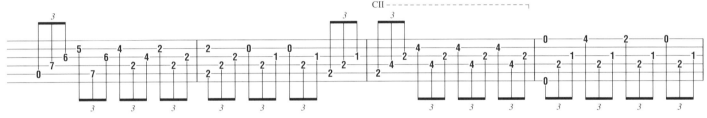

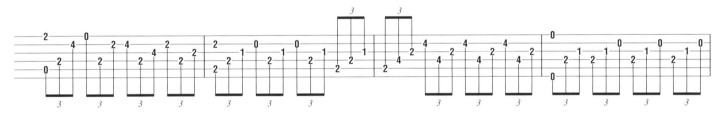

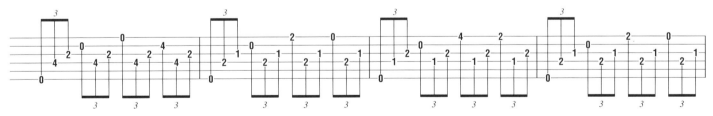

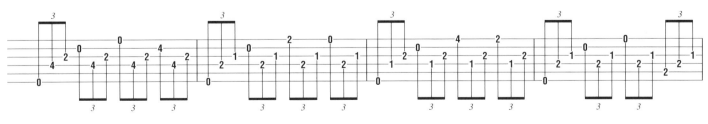

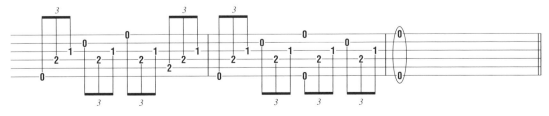

Vibrato

One technique that can really add some flair to your playing is vibrato. Vibrato added to a sustained note gives it a real singing quality. Watch the DVD for a demonstration.

So now that you can hear the difference, let's talk about the technique. In standard guitar, vibrato generally involves a more extreme shaking of the note, bending it up and down repeatedly. In classical guitar, however, vibrato tends to be more subtle. It's achieved with a lateral or sideways movement, along the length of the string, producing a subtle variation in pitch.

Vibrato isn't something you want to add to every note, but it's a nice effect when you have a note that holds for a bit. Try it here on this C major scale.

For our final piece, the popular "Romance in E Minor," by an anonymous 19th century composer, we'll combine all the techniques we studied in this lesson: fretted bass notes, arpeggios, barres, and vibrato.

"ROMANCE IN E MINOR"
Anonymous

Anonymous

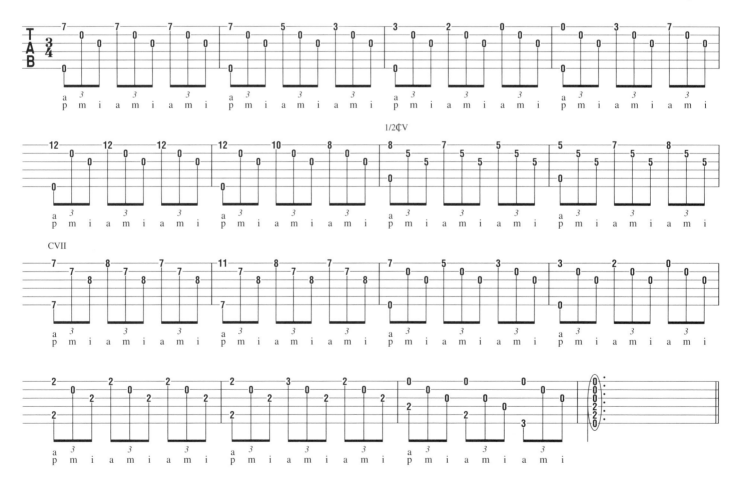

Well, that wraps up this lesson and the book. Remember, classical guitar requires discipline and practice, but it's an incredibly rewarding instrument. Good luck with your classical pursuits, and remember to have fun.